NEIGHBORS™

THE YARD CRITTERS TOO™

Library of Congress Control Number: 2012937095

ISBN: 978-0-916754-26-6

Printed and bound in Canada.

The text of this book is set in Ideal Sans Medium; title designs by Joung Un Kim.

The illustrations are rendered in collage.

Book design by Joung Un Kim.

Design Consultants:

Matteo Bologna, Mucca Design

Bryan Canniff, Bryan Canniff Designs

Educational Consultant:

Mary Ann Gioeli

Filsinger & Company, Ltd.

288 West 12 Street (Apt. 2R)

By appt.: 212-243-7421

New York, New York 10014, USA

www.filsingerco.com

First Edition 10 9 8 7 6 5 4 3 2 1

NEIGHBORS

THE YARD CRITTERS TOO

poems by GEORGE HELD

pictures by JOUNG UN KIM

Filsinger & Company, Ltd.
New York

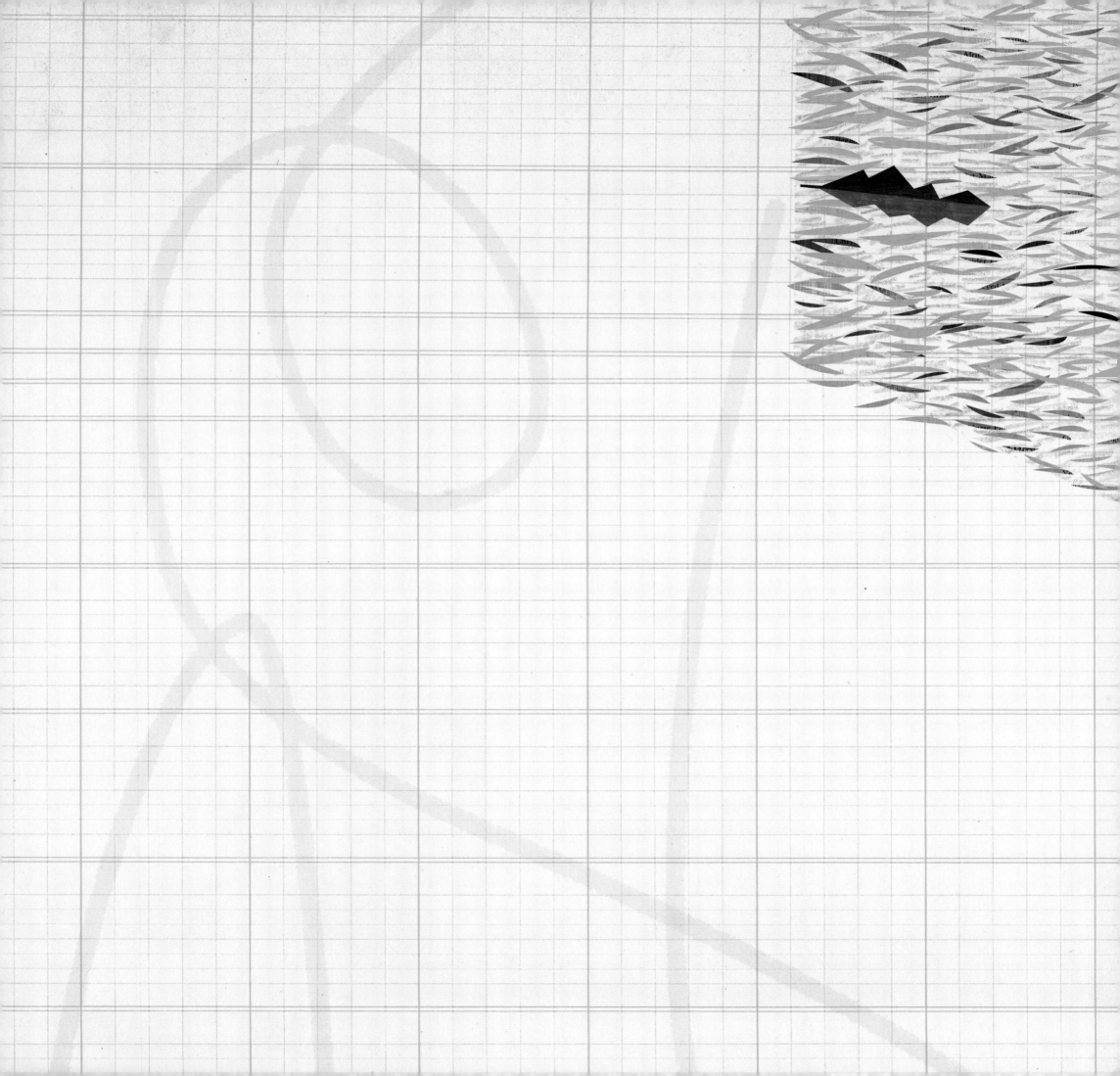

CONTENTS

LADYBUG LADYBUG

don't fly away,
fly away home:
your house is secure
and your children
well cared for.

Stay and play
with us, crawl
on our arm, stall
in elbow hollow,
spread wings,

but stay, don't
fly away, don't
leave us bereft,
without your crimson
dome with black dots,

your antennae,
the tickle of your
six feet on our
arm, your good luck
charm.

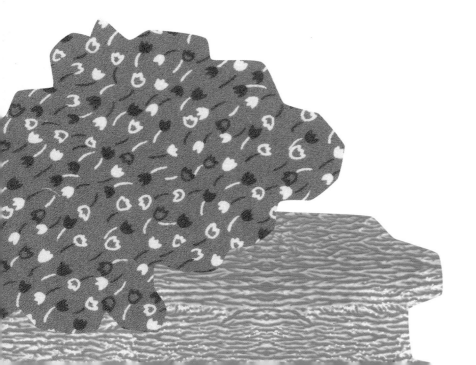

CRONY CROW

That big black crow,
feathery and bony,
has brains enough
to be your crony.

He can cawl out
to his playmates
on nearby boughs,
like you can to yours,

and summon them
for a powwow.
He can make more sense
than Schnauzer's bowwow.

His Blackness, as he
prefers to be called,
can learn human speech,
so don't be appalled

if your local crow
acts like he's loony –
he's not cartoony
and his brain's not slow.

Watch, listen, and grow
grateful for his show.

SPARROW

The sparrow
is narrow

she perches
on the rim
of a barrow

or flies
through the air
like an arrow

she never falls
to the earth
without God's sorrow

COYOTE

Coyote's not coy,
especially a boy;
he'll saunter into
your yard to

catch you off guard:
if you think
he's a doggie,
in less than a wink

he's off with your pet
rabbit in his jaws.
He's the wildest yet,
so give pause:

this brute's cute
but a trickster –
shout, don't be mute,
if he threatens your sister.

I wanna know who in the Western State of America a yellow dog.
What luck!

SHREW

Smallest
of mammals,
Shrew's hard
to view.

Though dim
of sight
she can
hear

and scent
well as
a dog
can.

Her fur's
feather-soft
like mole-
skin.

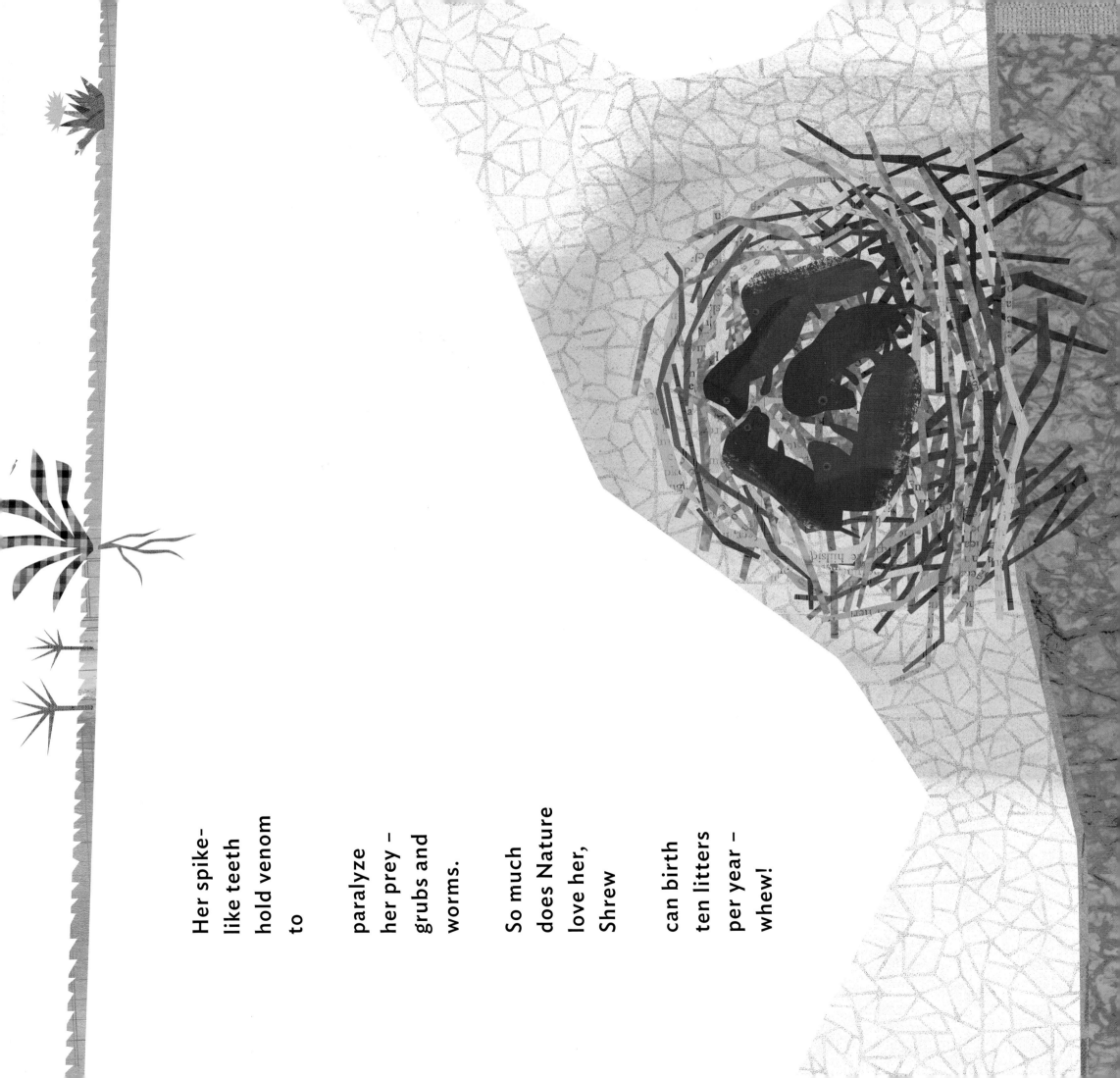

Her spike-
like teeth
hold venom
to

paralyze
her prey –
grubs and
worms.

So much
does Nature
love her, Shrew

can birth
ten litters
per year –
whew!

Speed Merchant (a riddle)

That wee startling birdie,
slim beak long as body –

hardly bigger than bumblebees,
whose darting ways it copies

at speeds faster than the breeze
among the flowers and trees –

hovers at red salvia cup
on whose nectar it will sup.

Sun gleams on ruby throat,
wings a blur at 90 beats

a second to loft 3 ounces;
heartbeat 1200 in duress.

Flying from Belize to bless our summer,
this ingenious gem is called the - - - - - -.

TICK

Tick's an anesthesiologist,
secreting in her spit
a numbing agent
so you can't feel her bite.

Tick nymph's a phlebotomist,
drawing blood to swell herself,
then falling off to molt
into an adult.

Tick's like Typhoid Mary,
infecting you with lyme
disease, so be wary
during play time

lest Tick in the grass
latch on you, and her eight
spider legs take her out of sight
to a spot where she'll bite.

To make sure you won't get sick,
let Mom check your body, even
'tween your toes, and tweeze out
that pencil point called Tick

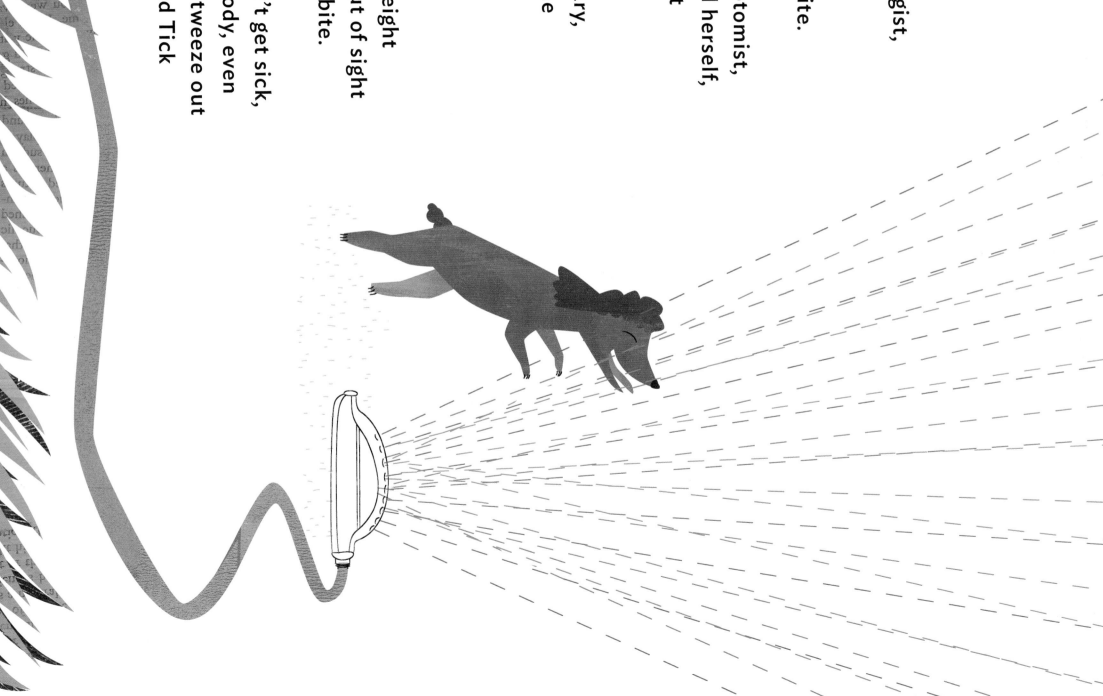

FIELD MOUSE

Sometimes in the field,
sometimes in the house,
most times ferrying ticks –
it's the field mouse!

She has good looks,
with white feet and belly,
but that scaly tail's
long as her body.

She'll eat anything
she fancies, indoors
or out, but has a long
list of predators,

like the carnivores
among her neighbors,
from cats to coyotes,
owls, snakes, and bears.

To survive, she's smart,
fast as a hummer
and bears a litter
every single month.

Owl

This nocturnal bird of prey
is less foul than fowl,
ever on the prowl
for mouse or vole.

His "spectacles" make him wise
in some folks' eyes
but mainly his wisdom
resides in his talons

so fit for grasping a meal,
so strong they quash a squeal.
Downy feathers stifle sound
as Owl dives from tree to ground

and lifts his prize to a branch
to swallow his midnight brunch.

SKUNK

No need for the skunk
to slink around the yard;
the threat of his stink
lets him parade

along the lawn
and dig a den
under the porch
where he'll scratch

on the wall at night
till he goes to sleep
for the winter.
Let him hibernate

in peace. Keep cat
and dog out of reach
lest their fur
need a chlorine bleach

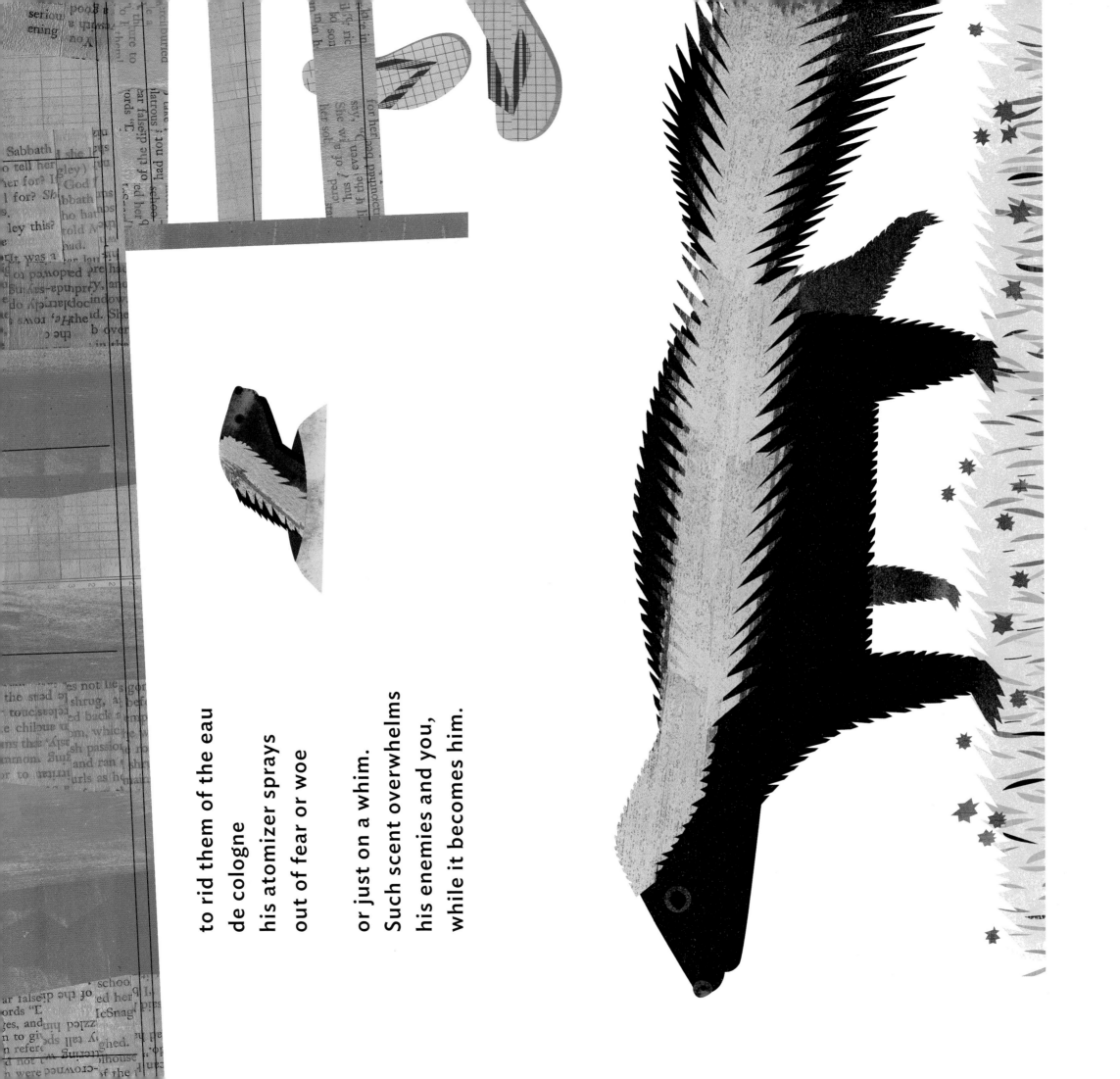

to rid them of the eau
de cologne
his atomizer sprays
out of fear or woe

or just on a whim.
Such scent overwhelms
his enemies and you,
while it becomes him.

PORCUPINE

It's a thrill
to see this
walking quill
cushion

strolling uphill
from the cellar
where he's built
a den down under.

That rattle is his quills
bouncing off
each other
unless he's still,

sniffing for swill
or predator.
Just wait till
he lumbers on or

darts his quilled tail
forward to ward off
your poodle –
then run to save

your pooch
from a snoot
full of pins
and needles,

and stay
out of range
of that strange
barbed way–

farer: his weapon's
worse than a skunk's.

CHIPMUNK

Cinnamon sides
with black stripes

a short broad tail
and squirrelly face

mark this handsome
rodent – yes, rodent –

like mouse or rat,
a morsel for the cat

we love these little critters
and wish them many litters

DISCOVER your NEIGHBORS

— Can you spot a mammal, an insect, a bird?

— Can you choose an animal? How does it move? What sounds does it make? Can you guess what it eats and what its home is like?

— Why do some animals TAKE our food and others HUNT for food?

— If you were an animal, which one would you be? And why?

— What is a wild animal / what is a pet?

Look for **NEIGHBORS**

THE WATER CRITTERS in 2014